MARGARET THATCHER

The Iron Lady

THE HISTORY HOUR

CONTENTS

❧ I ❧

INTRODUCTION

❦

If you want something said, ask a man; if you want something done, ask a woman.

    Margaret Thatcher

❦

Margaret Thatcher the girl from east London who grew to become the first female British prime minister and the first female minister in the whole of Europe. Her policies spearheaded the evolution of British economy and set it on the course of liberalism. She was by personality the first British woman to be renowned for her prowess in political leadership and administration which became known as 'Thatcherim'. The "iron lady" as she was often referred to as the leader of the British conservative party and three times British prime minister and was the only one in the 20th century to win three successive terms. During her tenure as Britain's prime minister, she used her position to cut social welfare programs, privatized major industries, and reduced trade union power. These policies greatly improved the economy of Britain. Margaret Thatcher showed commitment and bravery. She challenged and rose to fight the tyranny of the Soviet Union and criticised the leadership of Saddam Hussein, she also fought for the liberation of African countries and helped to end most of the civil wars that emerged during the 80s and 90s. She later resigned in 1999 after 12 years as British Prime Minister. She died at the age of 87 on April 8, 2013.

❧ II ❧

THE EARLY CHILDHOOD
OF THE IRON LADY

❦

The problem with socialism is that you eventually run
out of other peoples' money.
   Margaret Thatcher

❦

Margaret Thatcher was born Margaret Hilda Roberts on the
13th of October 1925 in Grantham, a small market town in the
southern district of Lincolnshire in England. Her parents
were Alfred Roberts and Beatrice Ethel. Alfred was a local
grocer and preacher who later became the Mayor of
Grantham. Margaret spent most of her early childhood
assisting her father with the family grocery business alongside
her sister Muriel. Her father Albert engaged in local politics
at the Finkin Street Methodist church in Grantham and

together with his wife, Beatrice brought up Margaret and Muriel to be dedicated Methodists. Margaret lived with her sister and parents in an apartment above her parent's grocery store on North Parade.

❦

In 1945 her father became the Mayor of Grantham but lost his position in 1952 as alderman to the labor party who had a majority in the Grantham Council. Seeing her father at a young age attaining a leadership position inspired the leadership in little Margaret. Her father introduced her to conservative politics as he was a member of the town's council from whom she first learned the conservative mindset that would later become a political force in British politics.

❦

Margaret had always had a conservative mindset. At the age of 12 she and her sister Muriel, saved their pocket allowances to assist in paying for the journey of a teenage Jewish girl who escaped from Germany before the Second World War. Her family gave shelter to the teenager throughout the period of the war.

MARGARET THATCHER GOES TO SCHOOL

❧

Margaret attended Huntingtower Road Primary School. She won a scholarship to continue her education at Kesteven and Grantham Girls School in 1936. She showed a serious commitment to her studies which was evident in her school reports. She was hardworking and also engaged in extracurricular activities like field hockey, piano, poetry recitals, walking, and swimming. Margaret demonstrated leadership qualities in school and was made the Head Girl in 1942 to 1943 academic year. She applied at Somerville College in Oxford to study chemistry in 1943. Somerville which was a college for women at the time rejected her application initially before offering her an admission after the withdrawal of another applicant.

❧

MARGARET SPENT four years studying chemistry at Somerville from 1943 to 1947. During this period she specialized in X-ray crystallography and did her dissertation on the structure of Gramicidin which is an antibiotic with Dorothy Hodgkin as her supervisor. Right from the onset she wasn't entirely devoted to studying chemistry because she was only interested in becoming a chemist for a while as she nurtured the desire to fulfill her lifelong dream of becoming a visionary political leader. While working as a chemist she constantly updated herself with the law and politics at that time. It was reported that she was more proud of the fact that she was the first British prime minister with a degree in science than that she was the first female prime minister.

❧

WHILE AT OXFORD she met Tony Bray a young man who was an army cadet. Tony was impressed by her unusual enthusiasm for politics which was uncommon among women at that time. He took a liking to Margaret immediately and on meeting her parents described her father as a "slightly austere" and "totally correct" man. Her mother he described as "motherly" and "very proper". Margaret and Tony became distant towards the end of her time at Oxford due to the fact that Tony's military training took him away from town more often. Tony hoped that the relationship fizzled-out as he thought Margaret had taken the relationship more serious than he did. When asked later in life about Tony Bray, Margaret while trying to evade the question acknowledges that they both had circumstances between them.

❧

MARGARET ROBERTS (THATCHER) became the president of the Oxford University Conservative Association in 1946. While at the university she was greatly influenced by "The

Road to Serfdom" (1944), which was the political work of Austrian – British philosopher and economist Friedrich Hayek, who was known for his fight for classical liberalism. Margaret was fascinated with "The Road to Serfdom" because it condemned the economic intervention by government as an antecedent to an authoritarian state.

᯾

SHE EARNED her Bachelor of Science (B.Sc) in Chemistry in 1947 with second-class honors. On completion of her program at Oxford, she moved to Colchester in Essex where she worked for BX Plastics close to Manningtree as a research chemist. While working in Essex she still nurtured a political ambition. She didn't allow her work stand in the way and joined the local conservative association. She was part of the representatives of the University Graduate Conservative Association that attended the party's conference in 1948 at Llandudno, Wales. Margaret rose to become a high ranking member of a popular organization of grassroots Conservative Party supporters with over 100,000 members known as "The Vermin Club". The group was formed as a response to an offensive comment made by Aneurin Bevan.

❦ III ❧

MARGARET THATCHER MAKES AN ENTRY INTO PUBLIC OFFICE

❦

Standing in the middle of the road is very dangerous; you get knocked down by the traffic from both sides.
   Margaret Thatcher

❦

Her first shot at public office came when a friend at Oxford introduced her to the chairman of the Dartford Conservative Association in Kent. Officials of the association who had been looking for candidates to represent the association in the upcoming elections were so impressed by her that they accepted her application even when she wasn't listed as a registered member on the association's list. In January of 1951, she was selected and included in the approved list.

On adoption, as the candidate for Dartford, she attended a dinner in February of 1951 where she met Denis Thatcher, a wealthy and successful businessman. At the end of the dinner, Denis drove her to the station to board a train to Essex.

Denis wasn't the first man Margaret was meeting after Tony Bray. She had met Willie Cullen a farmer who took a liking to her in 1949. Although she had gone on a series of dates with Cullen she was more interested in him meeting her sister Muriel. In one of her letter to Muriel, she wrote

> "went to the flicks yesterday with my farmer friend and got him all primed up to meet you sometime. I showed him the snapshot of you and I (sic) together – and he said he could scarcely tell the difference so I should think we could easily substitute me for you. When can you come down for a weekend? "

Muriel eventually came visiting in Colchester few weeks after Margaret and Willie began their relationship. Muriel was introduced to Willie who was still interested in the future prime minister. Willie lavished Margaret with expensive gifts such as a luxury bag that had her initials inscribed on it with the intention of winning her heart. However, Margaret was able to get Willie and Muriel together and the pair married in 1950.

MARGARET MEETS SIR DENIS
FOR THE FIRST TIME

❧

Margaret Roberts (Thatcher) moved to Dartford in order to prepare for the forthcoming elections. To support herself she worked at J. Lyons and Co. In Hammersmith as a research chemist who was part of a team working on suitable emulsifiers for ice cream. Deep down within her, Margaret knew it was almost impossible for her to win the position over the Liberal Partys candidate she still showed commitment to making a statement. She gained the respect of her peers in the political party with her speeches. Margaret attracted the attention of the media as she was the only female representative and the youngest one at that time. Although she lost the election twice to Norman Dodds she was able to reduce the majority of her opposition. During her campaigns, she was supported by her parents and Denis Thatcher who she later got married to in December of 1951. In one of her numerous letters to her sister Muriel whom she shared tales of her romance and foray into politics, Margaret described Denis as "a Major Thatcher, who has a flat in London (age about 36, plenty of money)....not a very attractive creature – very reserved but quite nice".

⚜

MARGARET DECIDED to study law at the Inns of Court School of Law in order to arm herself with the knowledge required to better shape her political ideology. Her husband Denis, sponsored her studies. The following year in 1953 she and Denis welcomed the birth of their twins Mark and Carol who she delivered prematurely through Caesarean section. After completing her Law degree, Margaret worked as a Lawyer and put politics aside to give her time to spend with her twins who were still little. She didn't contest in the 1955 general elections. After a few years, she decided it was time to get back into politics and searched for a winnable constituency. She was selected as the Conservative Partys candidate to represent Finchley in Parliament after narrowly defeating Ian Montagu Fraser in 1958.

MARGARET THATCHER BECOMES
A MEMBER OF PARLIAMENT

৩৯৩

S he was elected as a Member of Parliament to represent Finchley after a serious campaign in the 1959 general elections. Margaret in her maiden speech supported the Public Bodies Admission to Meetings Act 1960 which requires local authorities to have their meetings in public. The bill was successful and was passed into law. She went against her party when she voted for the restoration of birching as a Judicial Corporal Punishment (JCP) this showed that she wasn't going to be influenced by her party in changing her decisions relating to her job. Her motivation and drive made her to be mentioned as a potential prime minister even while in her 20s. She quickly debunked the possibility stating sometime in 1970, that

"there will not be a woman prime minister in my lifetime – the male population is too prejudiced".

❧

SHE GOT PROMOTED in October of 1961 by Harold Macmillan to the frontbench as Parliamentary Undersecretary at the Ministry of Pensions and National Insurance. She was among the first Members of parliament that were elected in 1959 to be promoted and was the youngest woman ever to attain such a post. She became the spokesman on housing and land matters after the Conservatives lost out in the 1964 elections. She used this position to promote her party's plan of permitting tenants to buy Council Houses that they lived in. In 1966 she went on to the Shadow Treasury team. As a spokesman for the treasury, she was against Labours mandatory price and income controls due to her belief that they will indeliberately yield efforts that will alter the economy. Party leaders soon began to see Margaret Thatcher as a likely Shadow Cabinet member. She was suggested by Jim Prior to being a member of the Shadow Cabinets but Chief Whip William Whitelaw and party leader Edward Heath agreed on Mervyn Pike to be the only woman member in the Shadow Cabinet. At the Conservative Party Conference in 1966, she condemned the Labour Governments high-tax policies and described them as a move "not only towards Socialism but towards Communism". She argued that lower tax discouraged hard work. She was also one of few Conservative Members of Parliament who supported David Steels bill to make abortion legal. She also voted in favor of the ban on hare coursing. She also voted against the lessening of divorce laws but was in support of the continuation of capital punishment.

❧

THATCHER WAS CHOSEN in 1967 by the United States

Embassy in London to participate in a professional exchange programme known as International Visitors Leadership Program (known then as the Foreign Leader Program). This programme provided her with the prospect of spending close to six weeks visiting a couple of US cities and institution where she met various political figures. One of such institutions as the IMF (International Monetary Fund). Although she wasn't yet a member of the Shadow Cabinet, the embassy went on to inform the State Department that she was a future Prime Minister. This description by the embassy made it possible for Margaret Thatcher to meet with top persons at a busy programme that was focused on issues relating to the economy. These top persons included Paul Samuelson, Nelson Rockefeller, Pierre-Paul Schweitzer and Walt Rostow. After the meeting, party leader Edward Heath appointed Margaret to the Shadow Cabinet as spokesman for fuel and power. Before the general elections in 1970, she was promoted twice, first to Shadow Transport spokesman and then to Education.

ON THE 20TH of April 1968, Enoch Powell who was a British member of parliament addressed a gathering of the Conservative Political Centre in Birmingham. In his speech, he criticised the proposed Race Relations Bill at that time and also the mass immigration into the United Kingdom. His speech caused a lot of uproars which was later termed the "Rivers of Blood" due to a quote he used in his speech. Powell instantly became the most divisive and talked about politician in the country. His remarks against immigration earned him a dismissal from the Shadow Cabinet by party leader of the Conservatives Edward Heath. Margaret Recalled that when heath informed her on the phone that he was going to sack Enoch Powell she actually "thought that it was better for things to cool down during the present rather than heighten the crisis". She felt that his beliefs about the Commonwealth immigration were right and that he was being misquoted in his speech.

MARGARET THATCHER EMERGES
AS SECRETARY OF STATE

৩৯৩

I n 1970, the Conservative Party won the general elections and Margaret was appointed as the Secretary of State for Education and Science. On resumption of her new office, she immediately attracted the attention of the public due to governments' attempts to reduce spending. She prioritized the academic needs in schools and calling on the need to cut down on administrative public expenditure on the state educational system. This resulted in the eradication of free milk for school children between the ages of seven and eleven. She maintained that some children will be affected if schools were charged for the provision of milk but agreed on the provision of a one-quarter pint daily to younger children for a nutritional purpose. This earned Margaret the name "Thatcher the Milk Snatcher". Papers revealed later by the Cabinet showed that she was against the policy but was pushed to support it by the treasury. Her abolition of free milk in the educational system was met with massive protest from the press and Labour. She revealed later in her biography that she considered quitting politics due to the uproar that followed her decision "I learned a valuable lesson. I had incurred the maximum political odium for the minimum of political benefit" she said.

⚜

MARGARET THATCHER WAS in full support of Lord Rothschilds proposal for market forces to influence government spending on research in 1971. The department examined the bid for more local education authorities to end grammar school and to accept comprehensive secondary education. She remained committed to operating a secondary modern-grammar school system of education in stages and tried to retain grammar schools. As the education secretary, she refused on 326 out of 3,612 bids for schools to turn into comprehensive schools. The percentage of pupils who attended comprehensive schools increased from 32% to 62% during her tenure.

⚜

EDWARD HEATH'S leadership of the Conservative party enabled him to form the "Heath Ministry" and was appointed by Queen Elizabeth II as the Prime Minister of the United Kingdom on the 19th of June 1970 a day after the general elections. Heaths Ministry experienced challenges with union demand for an increase in wages and oil embargoes in 1973. On losing the general elections in February 1974, Labour created a minority government that went on to win the October 1974 general elections by a narrow majority. As time went on it was unlikely that Edward Heath was going to remain the leader of the Conservative Party. Although Margaret wasn't initially seen as a likely replacement, she later became the likely contender with the promise of a fresh start. She won the first ballot over Heath and he resigned his position as the leader of the party. She defeated Whitelaw in the second ballot. Margaret's victory in the party leadership election divided the party as a majority of her support came from Members of Parliament to the right and also from those who were from South England, as well as those who did not attend public schools or Oxford and Cambridge.

THE IRON LADY IS LEADER OF
THE OPPOSITION

❦

Margaret Thatcher became the leader of the Conservative Party and thus leader of the opposition on February 11, 1975. She chose Whitelaw as her deputy while Heath was never in support of Thatcher's leadership of the party.

❦

THATCHER WAS an occasional visitor at the Institute of Economic Affairs (IAE), founded by Anthony Fisher. She had been a regular visitor and ardent reader of its publications since the early 1960s. At the IAE, she was influenced by the suggestions of Arthur Seldon and Ralph Harris, and soon became the forerunner of the ideological movement which opposed the British welfare state. They believed that the Keynesian economics was a stumbling block to the progress of Britain. The institute produced pamphlets which proposed lower taxes, less government and more freedom for consumers and business.

৩১৫৩

AFTER BEING CRITICISED for her presentation in the first ballot by TV critic Clive James, Thatcher was advised by Gordon Reece to work on her presentation which she did. She sought the help of actor Laurence Olivier through the help of Reece who arranged for voice coaching lessons for Thatcher. She was able to suppress her Lincolnshire dialect well enough and only found it difficult to suppress when she was under stress. This was evident in the House of Commons in 1983 when she was provoked by Denis Healey and accused the Labour Frontbench of being frit.

৩১৫৩

AS THE LEADER of the opposition, Thatcher was strongly against the creation of a Scottish assembly. She ordered Conservative MPs not to vote in support of the Scotland and Wales bill in December 1976. The bill was eventually defeated and when new bills were proposed, she was in support of the amendment of the legislation to allow the English to vote in the 1979 referendum on Scottish devolution.

৩১৫৩

BRITAIN'S ECONOMY suffered greatly in the 1970s that foreign secretary James Callaghan cautioned his fellow Labour Cabinet members of the chances of a breakdown of democracy, hinting them that "if I were a young man I would emigrate." Around 1978, the economy of Britain began to recover and opinion polls proved that Labour was in the lead. The general elections were round the corner and there were possibilities of Labour emerging as the winner. It came as a surprise to many when Prime Minister Callaghan announced on September 7 that there would be no general elections that year. He, however, proposed to go to the polls the following year in 1979. In reaction to this, Thatcher called the Labour government "chickens", she also got the backing of Liberal Party leader David Steel who criticised the Labour Party for "running scared".

❦

DURING THE WINTER of 1978 to 1979, the Labour government was faced with public criticism about the direction of the country which resulted in a series of strikes and protests, which was later referred to as the "winter of discontent". The conservative party challenged the Labour government's inability to create employment, utilizing media adverts with the slogan "Labour isn't working". In early 1979, Callaghan ministry lost a motion of no confidence and a general election was called for. The Conservative Party won 44-seats in the House of Commons. With the conservative having the majority of seats, Margaret Thatcher became the first female British Prime Minister.

❦

THATCHER MADE a foreign policy speech in 1976 where she criticized the Soviet Union for pursuing "world dominance". The Soviet Army journal "Krasnaya Zvezda" (Red Star) challenged her opinion in a story titled "Iron Lady Raises Fears" written by Captain Yuri Gavrilov. The next day, British newspaper The Sunday Time covered the story written by the

Soviet Army journal. A week later, Thatcher made reference to the publication in a speech to Finchley conservatives where she likened it to the Duke of Wellington's nickname "The Iron Duke". Thatcher was however referred to as the "Iron Lady" all through her political career.

❦ IV ❧

MARGARET THATCHER TAKES ON THE ROLE AS PRIME MINISTER

❦

I am extraordinarily patient, provided I get my own way in the end.

Margaret Thatcher

❦

Thatcher arrived at Downing Street as the Prime Minister of Britain on May 4, 1979. Upon her arrival, she paraphrased the prayer of Saint Francis.

"Where there is discord, may we bring harmony; Where there is error, may we bring truth; where there is doubt, may we bring faith; and where there is despair, may we bring hope.

Margaret Thatcher however at this time didn't know that she would remain in office all through the 1980s and would become the most powerful woman in the world.

❧

Margaret Thatcher became the Prime Minister of Britain at a period of increased racial anxiety in Britain. In a meeting with Foreign Secretary Lord Carrington and Home Secretary William Whitelaw in July 1979, she was against the number of Asian immigrants, with the aim of reducing the total of Vietnamese boat people permitted to settle in the United Kingdom to less than 10,000 over a period of two years.

❧

As British Prime Minister, Thatcher visited Queen Elizabeth II weekly to talk about governance. Her relationship with the Queen came under serious scrutiny. Her biographer John Campbell wrote that

"one question that continued to fascinate the public about the phenomenon of a woman Prime Minister was how she got on with the Queen. The answer is that their relations were punctiliously correct, but there was little love lost on either side. As two women of very similar age – Mrs. Thatcher was six months older – occupying a parallel position at the top of the social pyramid, one the head of government, the other head of state, they were bound to be in some sense rivals. Mrs. Thatcher's attitude to the Queen was ambivalent. On the one hand, she had an almost mystical reverence for the institution of the monarchy: she always made sure that Christmas dinner was finished in time for everyone to sit down solemnly to watch the Queen's broadcast. Yet at the same time, she was trying to modernize the country and sweep away many of the values and practices which the monarchy perpetuated.

❧

Thatcher herself wrote,

"I have always found the Queen's attitude towards the work of the Government absolutely correct... stories of clashes between 'two powerful women' were just too good not to make up."

❧

As leader of the government, Thatcher's policies were influenced by economists and monetarists thinking like that of Alan Walters and Milton Friedman. In collaboration with Geoffrey Howe the Chancellor of the Exchequer, Thatcher reduced direct taxes on income and increased indirect taxes. She reduced inflation by increasing the interest rates to reduce the growth of money in circulation. She introduced cash limits on public spending and lowered expenditure on social services like housing and education. Reductions to higher education made her become the first Oxford-trained post-war Prime Minister who didn't have an honorary doctorate from Oxford University, after a 738 − 319 vote of the governing Congress and a student petition.

❧

Thatcher's newly introduced City Technology Colleges didn't

achieve its desired success. The funding agency was introduced to control expenditure by opening and closing schools. It was described as having "an extraordinary range of dictatorial powers". There were some Conservatives in the Cabinet who were loyal to Heath who expressed doubts over Thatcher's policies. The England riot of 1981 prompted the British media to discuss the need for a policy U-turn. Thatcher dealt with the issue during the Conservative Party conference in 1980, she made a speech using phrases originally written by Ronald Millar which included the lines-

"You turn if you want to. The Lady's not for turning!"

❧

As time went on Thatcher's job approval rating dropped to 23% by the end of 1980, which was the lowest recorded for any of the previous Prime Ministers before her. She increased taxes as the recession of the early 1980s worsened which was against concerns expressed in a March 1981 statement which was signed by 364 leading economists. By 1981, there was a sign of economic recovery in the UK, inflation was reduced to 8.6% from 18% but unemployment rose to over 3 million for the first time since the 1930s. By the year 1983, there was a strengthened growth in the economy, and mortgage and inflation rates had declined to their lowest levels in 13 years. While there was a drop in the manufacturing employment as a share of total employment to over 30%, the total unemployment remained high with 3.3 million recorded in 1984.

BRITAIN HAS GOT A NEW
ECONOMIC HERO

❀

B y the year 1987, unemployment rate reduced,
inflation was low and the economy was strong and
stable. Opinion polls revealed a comfortable Conservative lead, and there was also a success in the local council
elections. This prompted Thatcher to call for a general election which was slated for June 11 of the same year, even when
the deadline for an election was still 12 months ahead. The
success of Conservatives at the election gave Thatcher her
Third successive term.

❀

MARGARET THATCHER WAS against British membership to
the Exchange Rate Mechanism (ERM), which was a pioneer
in the European Monetary Union. She believed that it would
restrict the British economy, irrespective of the urge from
both Nigel Lawson her Chancellor of the Exchequer and
Geoffrey Howe who was Foreign Secretary. She was

persuaded by Lawson's successor as Chancellor in October 1990 to join the ERM at what was said to be too high a rate.

❧

MARGARET THATCHER MADE changes to local government taxes by substituting domestic rates with a new community charge, in which the same amount was charged to every adult resident. The new tax policy was first introduced in Scotland in 1989 and later in Wales and England the next year, and was among the least accepted policies of her leadership. This led to an over 200,000 strong public demonstration in March 1990 in London. The public protest around Trafalgar Square resulted in riots which led to the injury of 113 people and the arrest of 340 persons. The community charge was later removed by her successor, John Major in 1991.

❧

THATCHER SAW the trade unions as a danger to both the public and ordinary trade unionist. She was determined to reduce the power of the unions, whose leadership she blamed for undermining economic performance and parliamentary democracy through strike actions. A host of unions embarked on strike actions in reply to legislation introduced to reduce their power, but resistance eventually dwindled. In the 1983 general elections, only 309% of union members voted for Labour. Quoting the BBC in 2004, Thatcher had "managed to destroy the power of the trade unions for almost a generation". The biggest face-off between the unions and the government under Margaret Thatcher was the miners' strike of 1984 to 1985.

❧

THE NATIONAL COAL Board (NCB) in March 1984, incited to close down 20 of the 174 government-owned mines and terminate 20,000 jobs out of 187,000. More than half of the country's miners guided by the National Union of Mineworkers (NUM) under Arthur Scargill, refused to work and embarked on a strike action. Scargill rejected the move to hold a ballot on the strike action, due to the fact that he had lost three ballots on a national strike. As a result of Scargill's refusal to hold a ballot, the High Court of Justice declared the strike action as illegal.

⚜

THATCHER STOOD her grounds and refused to heed to the union's demands and likened the miner's disagreement to the Falklands conflict, this she said in a speech in 1984. "We had to fight the enemy without in the Falklands. We always have to be aware of the enemy within, which is much more difficult to fight and more dangerous than liberty". In March 1985 after a year of strike action, the leadership of the NUM conceded without an agreement. The financial cost of the strike action to the economy was close to £1.5 billion, the strike action led to the fall of the pounds against the dollar. The state closed 25 unprofitable coal mines in 1985, and by the year 1992, 97 coals mines had seized to operate and were closed down and those that were remaining were privatized by the year 1994.

⚜

THE CLOSURE of 150 coal mines, some of which were not recording losses resulted in the loss of jobs in tens of thousands and had a devastating effect on entire communities. The strike actions brought down Heath's government, and

Thatcher was committed to succeeding where Heath failed. Thatcher strategy in winning over the striking miners was by preparing fuel stocks, appointing disciplinarian Ian MacGregor as NCB leader and making sure that the police was adequately trained and equipped with the necessary gears to handle riots. In 1979, the number of stoppages across the United Kingdom rose to 4,583 when over 29 million working days had been lost. During the miner's strike in 1984, the number of stoppages was 1,221 which resulted in the loss of over 27 million working days. Throughout the remainder of Thatcher's premiership stoppages reduce drastically. In 1990 there was 630 stoppages and less than 2 million working days lost, and this number continues to dwindle as time went on. During Thatcher reign as Prime Minister, there was a notable decline in trade union density, with the percentage of workers who belong to a trade union reducing from 57.3% in 1979 to 49.5% in 1985. From Thatcher's assumption of office in 1979 till when she left, the membership of trade unions dropped from 13.5 million to less than 10 million.

THATCHER WAS a great supporter of privatization; she saw it as a way to reduce government operation of services. The sale of government utilities increased after the 1983 general elections. Over £29 billion was realized from the privatization of state industries, and another £18 billion was realized from the sales of council houses. The smooth sale of state industries was brought about by the improvement in performance of the economy especially in the areas of labor productivity. Some of the industries that were privatized included water, electricity, and gas, were natural monopolies for which the sales of these industries did not result in an increase in competition. Regulations and laws were also increased to make up for the loss of direct government control on these industries. Regulatory bodies such as Oftel, Ofgas, and the National Rivers Authority were established. The privatization of industries benefitted consumers by way of lower prices for goods and services and improved efficiency in privatized industries. Thatcher, however, was against the privatization of British Rail and was reported to have told Nicholas Ridley who then Transport Secretary that

---

"Railway privatization will be the Waterloo of this government. Please never mention the railways to me again".

Before her resignation as Prime Minister in 1990, she agreed to the calls for privatizing the British Rail which John Major her successor implemented in 1994. The privatization of state assets was joined with financial deregulation in a bid to increase economic growth. The UK exchange controls were abolished by Chancellor Geoffrey Howe in 1979, which created more room for capital investment in foreign markets. The big bang (sudden deregulation of the financial market) removed many hindrances on the London Stock Exchange.

৯৯৯

IN 1980 AND 1981, the Provisional Irish Republican Army (PIRA) and Irish Liberation Army (INLA) in Maze Prison situated in Northern Ireland engaged in hunger strikes in an attempt to regain the rank of political prisoners who had been removed in 1976 by the heralding Labour government. Bobby Sands started the hunger strike in 1981 saying that he would fast till death except prison inmates won recognition

over their living conditions. Thatcher declined to agree to a return to political status for the prisoners. Saying that "crime is crime; it is not political". Nonetheless, the British government secretly contacted Republican leaders in a quest to end the hunger strike. After the death of Bobby Sands and nine other prisoners, the strike came to an end. Paramilitary prisoners were accorded some rights, but not an official recognition of political status. During the period of the hunger strike by prisoners, there was an increase in violence in Northern Ireland.

෴

MARGARET THATCHER ESCAPED an assassination attempt by the IRA at a Brighton hotel on the morning of October 12, 1984. Unfortunately, five people were killed in the assassination attempt including the wife of Minister John Wakeham. Thatcher stayed at the hotel in Brighton in preparation for the Conservative Party conference, which she insisted must hold the following day even after the attempts on her life. She delivered her speech as scheduled, although it was a rewrite of her original draft based on the circumstances. The move to go ahead with the planned conference was widely supported by different political spectrum and this increased her popularity among the public. On November 6, 1981, Margaret Thatcher and Garret Fitzgerald created the Anglo-Irish Inter-Governmental Council, a forum with the aim of serving as a meeting point for both governments. Four years later on November 15, 1985, Thatcher and Fitzgerald signed the Hillsborough Anglo-Irish Agreement, which was the first time a British Government had accorded the Republic of Ireland an advisory role in the administration of Northern Ireland. Ian Pasley led the Ulster Says No movement in protest in Belfast. The protesters were over 100,000. Ian Gow who was later assassinated by the PIRA resigned his position as Minister of State in the HM Treasury, and the entire 15 unionist Members of Parliament (MPs) resigned their seat in parliament.

ॐ

THATCHER WAS in support of an active climate protection policy and was a chief proponent of the passing of the Environmental Protection Act in 1990. She was also in support of the establishment of the Intergovernmental Panel on Climate Change, and in founding the Hadley Centre for Climate Research and Prediction. She assisted in including acid rain, climate change and pollution in the British mainstream towards the end of the 1980s. In 1989 Thatcher called for a global treaty on climate change. This she made known in her September 27, 1988, speech to the Royal Society and her November 1989 speech to the UN General Assembly. When she retired as Prime Minister in 1990 she was however unsure about the climate change policy and refused climate alarmism (media coverage of global warming).

THE IRON LADY RESCUES
ZIMBABWE FROM RACISM

⚜

L ord Carrington was appointed by Thatcher as Foreign Minister in 1979. Before his appointment as Foreign Minister, Carrington was the Minister of Defence and a senior member of the party. Lord Carrington tried to avoid domestic affairs and was in good terms with Thatcher. First on the agenda was how to solve the Rhodesia problem. The issue with Rhodesia at the time was partly racial, in which the 5% white population was bent on ruling the prosperous, largely black former colony. This sparked an overwhelming international condemnation of the act. After the end of the Portuguese Empire in Africa in 1975, Rhodesia chief supporter – South Africa, discovered that the country was a liability. A black rule was eminent and Carrington nego-tiated a harmonious solution to the problem at the Lancaster House conference in December 1979. In attendance at the conference were Prime Minister of Rhodesia Ian Smith and also major black leaders such as Robert Mugabe, Joshua

Nkomo, Josiah Tongogara and Abel Muzorewa. The conference brought an end to the Rhodesian bush war (also known
as the Zimbabwean war of freedom) and led to the creation
of the new nation of Zimbabwe under a black rule in 1980.

MARGARET THATCHER'S INFLUENCES FOREIGN POLICIES

❁

Power is like being a lady... if you have to tell people you are, you aren't.

Margaret Thatcher

❁

Thatcher's first foreign policy crisis was at the 1979 USSR invasion of Afghanistan. She damned the invasion, saying it showed the bankruptcy of a faulty policy and assisted in convincing some British athletes not to attend the 1980 Moscow Olympics. She wasn't in total support of the president of the United States Jimmy Carter who attempted to rebuke the USSR with economic sanctions. Britain's economic situation was unstable, and most of NATO hesitated in cutting trade ties. The Financial Times reported that

Thatcher's government was secretly supporting Saddam Hussein with military gears since 1981.

❧

Thatcher became a close supporter of the Cold War policies of US President Ronald Reagan, based on their collective disbelieve of Communism. A disagreement ensued in 1983 when Ronald Reagan did not seek her consent on the invasion of Grenada. During her first 12 months as Prime Minister she was in support of NATO's decision to set up US nuclear cruise and Pershing II missiles in Western Europe, allowing the US to position more than 160 cruise missiles at RAF Greenham Common, beginning on November 14, 1983, and inciting a rowdy protest by the Campaign for Nuclear Disarmament. Thatcher bought the Trident nuclear missile submarine from the US to substitute Polaris, which tripled the UK's nuclear forces at a cost of over £12 billion (which was the price at 1996). Thatcher's fondness for defense alliance with the US was glaring in the Westland affair of 1985–1986, when she collaborated with colleagues to permit the pressurized helicopter manufacturer Westland to reject a takeover bid from the Italian firm Agusta in support of the management's favorite option, a connection with Sikorsky Aircraft. Secretary of Defence Michael Heseltine, who had consented to the Agusta deal, resigned from the government in disagreement.

❧

THATCHER RESCUES THE
FALKLANDS

෨෨

On April 2, 1982, the leading military junta in
Argentina gave the go-ahead to the invasion of the
British possessions of the Falkland Islands and
South Georgia, which sparked the Falklands War. The crises
that followed was "a defining moment of her [Thatcher's]
premiership". At the suggestion of Robert Armstrong and
Harold Macmillian, Thatcher instituted and led a small War
Cabinet (formally called ODSA, Overseas and Defence
committee, South Atlantic) to supervise the conduct of the
war, which by 5–6 April had endorsed and dispatched a naval
task force to recapture the islands.

෨෨

ARGENTINA SURRENDERED on June 14 and Operation Corpo-
rate was seen as a success, even though 255 British servicemen
and 3 Falkland Islanders died during the period of the war.
Argentine fatalities stood at 649, half of them passed away

after the nuclear-powered submarine HMS Conqueror torpe-
doed and sank the cruiser ARA General Belgrano on May
2.Thatcher was condemned for the disregard of the Falklands'
defence that resulted in the war, and particularly by Tam
Dalyell in Parliament for the resolution to torpedo the
General Belgrano, but altogether, Thatcher was seen as a
highly effective and committed war leader. The "Falklands
factor", an economic recovery started early in 1982, and a
cynically divided opposition all played a key part in Thatcher's second victory in the 1983 general elections. Thatcher
was occasionally referred after the war as the "Falklands
spirit" journalists Simon Jenkins and Max Hastings recommended in 1983 that this reflected her fondness for the
streamlined decision-making of her War Cabinet over the
difficult task of promoting a peacetime cabinet government.

SHE SIGNS A TREATY WITH THE CHINESE

❦

In September 1982, Thatcher visited China to meet with Deng Xiaoping the sovereignty of Hong Kong after 1997. China was the first communist state that Margaret Thatcher had visited and she was also the first prime minister of Britain to visit China. During the course of their meeting, she required the PRC's agreement for the British to remain in the territory. Deng maintained that the PRC's sovereignty on Hong Kong wasn't debatable, but declared his readiness to settle the sovereignty problem with the British government with the help of formal negotiations, and both governments agreed to preserve Hong Kong's stability and prosperity. After negotiating for a period of 2 years, Thatcher succumbed to the PRC government and signed the Sino-British Joint Declaration in 1984 in Beijing, with the agreement to hand over Hong Kong's sovereignty in 1997.

THATCHER IS AN ENEMY OF
APARTHEID

❦

I n April 1986 she allowed US F-111s to utilize Royal Air
Force bases for the bombing of Libya in response for
the alleged Libyan bombing of a Berlin discothèque,
citing the right of self-defense under Article 51 of the UN
Charter. Polls recommended that less than one in three
British citizens approved of her decision.

❦

IT BECAME obvious that she was in support of "peaceful negotiations" to bring an end to apartheid, Thatcher was against
sanctions imposed on South Africa by the Commonwealth
and the European Economic Community (EEC).[She tried to
preserve trade with South Africa while convincing the
government there to ditch apartheid. This involved parading
herself as President Botha's bosom friend, and requesting
that he visits the UK in 1984, irrespective of the unavoidable
demonstrations against his government. Thatcher discharged

the African National Congress (ANC) in October 1987 as "a typical terrorist organization". When he visited Britain five months after his release from prison, Nelson Mandela commended Thatcher saying:

"She is an enemy of apartheid ... We have much to thank her for."

ॐ

THATCHER and her government supported the Khmer Rouge retaining their seat in the UN after they were removed from power in Cambodia by the Cambodian–Vietnamese War. Although Thatcher never agreed to it at the time, it was discovered in 1991 that since 1983 the SAS had secretly ordered for the training of the "non-Communist" members of the CGDK to fight against the Kampuchea (PRK) government which was supported by the vietnamese. Non-communist members such as the Khmer People's National Liberation Front and the Sihanoukists were subjugated, diplomatically and militarily, by the Khmer Rouge. It was reported that the SAS had trained them on how to use improvised explosive devices, booby traps and to manufacture and use time-delay devices, in what activist Rae McGrath rejected as a criminally irresponsible and cynical policy.

ॐ

THATCHER and her party were in support of British membership of the EEC in the 1975 national referendum, but she thought that the role of the organization should be restricted to guarantee free trade and valuable competition, and panicked that the EEC's methods were at odds with her stand on smaller government and deregulation. Her resistance to further European integration became more noticeable during her premiership and especially after her third victory at the 1987 general election. At a speech in Bruges in 1988, she summarized her disapproval to proposals from the EEC, predecessor of the European Union, for a federal structure and heightened centralization of decision making. She made this clear by stating that, "We have not successfully rolled back the frontiers of the state in Britain, only to see them re-imposed at a European level, with a European super-state exercising a new dominance from Brussels."

۞

MARGARET THATCHER WAS one of the pioneer Western leaders to respond kindly to reformist USSR leader Mikhail Gorbachev. Taking into consideration findings from the Reagan–Gorbachev summit meetings and reforms enacted by Gorbachev in the USSR, she declared in November 1988 that "We're not in a Cold War now", but rather in a "new relationship much wider than the Cold War ever was". She went on a state visit to the USSR in 1984 and met with Gorbachev and chairman of Council of Ministers Nikolai Ryzhkov.

۞

THATCHER WAS in the United States on a working visit when Iraqi leader Saddam Hussein attacked neighboring Kuwait in August 1990. At her meetings with President George H. W. Bush, who succeeded Reagan in 1989, she suggested an intervention, and pressurized Bush to send troops to the Middle East to pursue the Iraqi Army out of Kuwait. Bush was hesitant about the plan, causing Thatcher to say to him during a telephone conversation that "This was no time to go wobbly!" Thatcher's government sent military forces to the international coalition in the climax of the Gulf War, but she had resigned by the time conflict began on 17 January 1991. She commended the coalition victory as a backbencher, but cautioned that "the victories of peace will take longer than the battles of war". It was later discovered that Thatcher recommended frightening Saddam with chemical weapons after the attack on Kuwait.

❦

THATCHER, sharing the worries of President of France François Mitterrand, was originally in contrast to German reunification, telling Gorbachev that it "would lead to a change to postwar borders, and we cannot allow that because such a development would undermine the stability of the whole international situation and could endanger our security". She made known her worries that a united Germany would support itself better with the Soviet Union and deviate from NATO. In March 1990, the Chancellor of West German Helmut Kohl made it clear to Thatcher that he would keep her "informed of all his intentions about unification", and that he was ready to reveal "matters which even his cabinet would not know". In November 1989, Thatcher commended the fall of the Berlin Wall as "a great day for freedom".

THATCHER'S PUBLIC RATING
DECLINES

౭৵৪

T hatcher was in contention for the leadership of the
Conservative Party by Sir Anthony Meyer who was
an unpopular backbench MP in the 1989 leadership
election. Of the 374 Conservative MPs who were capable of
voting, 314 voted for Thatcher and 33 for Meyer. Her
followers in the party saw the result as a success and were
against suggestions that there was dissatisfaction within
the party.

౭৵৪

DURING HER TENURE as British Prime Minister, Thatcher
got the second-lowest average approval rating (40%) of any
post-war Prime Minister. After the resignation of Nigel
Lawson as Chancellor in October 1989, polls constantly
showed that her party was more popular. A self-described
passionate politician, Thatcher always maintained that she

didn't care much about her ratings at the poll and was more comforted instead by her unbeaten election record.

❦

OPINION POLLS CONDUCTED in September 1990 showed that Labour Party had gained a 14% lead over the Conservatives, and by November the Conservatives had been following Labour closely for 18 months. These ratings, in addition to Thatcher's aggressive personality and penchant to dominate collegiate opinion, contributed to dissatisfaction within the Conservative party.

❦

THATCHER DISMISSED Geoffrey Howe as Foreign Secretary in July 1989 after he and Lawson had coerced her to accept a plan for Britain to be part of the European Exchange Rate Mechanism (ERM). Britain became part of the ERM in October 1990. On November 1, 1990, Howe, by now was the last remaining member of Thatcher's initial 1979 cabinet, resigned from his position as Deputy Prime Minister, apparently over her open resentment to plans towards European Monetary Union. In his resignation speech on November 13, Howe commented on Thatcher's openly dismissive attitude to the government's suggestion for a new European currency challenging against established currencies (a "hard ECU")

❧ VI ❧
MARGARET THATCHER RESIGNS AS PRIME MINISTER

❧

You may have to fight a battle more than once to win it.

Margaret Thatcher

❧

Howe's resignation brought a speedy end to Thatcher's reign as Prime Minister.

❧

On November 14, Michael Heseltine placed a bid for the leadership of the Conservative Party. Opinion polls had shown that he would present the Conservatives an opportunity to lead over Labour in the polls. Even though Thatcher had succeeded in winning the first ballot with a vote of 204 to 152 with 16 abstentions, Heseltine had garnered enough support to compel the second ballot. Under party rules, Thatcher needed to win a majority vote, with a margin that was at least equal to 15% of the 372 Conservative MPs in order to win the leadership election entirely. However, she won with a margin of 54.8% while Haseltine had 40.9% vote, she needed four votes to win by a margin of 15%. Thatcher at first made it known that she was willing to "fight on and fight to win" the second ballot, but after consulting with her close cabinet members and associate she was persuaded to withdraw from the second ballot. After meeting with the queen, and speaking with other world leaders, and making one last Commons speech, she resigned her position as the Prime Minister on 28 November. On her exit from Downing Street, She apparently regarded her exit as a betrayal. Her resignation came as a shock to many outside Britain, with foreign observers like Henry Kissinger and Gorbachev discreetly showing concerns.

❦

Chancellor John Major replaced Thatcher as party leader and Prime Minister, who triumphed over Heseltine in the following ballot. Major oversaw an improvement in Conservative support in the 17 months period that led to the 1992 general election and took the party to a fourth consecutive victory on April 9, 1992. Thatcher supported Major in the leadership contest, but her support for him declined as time went on.

❦

Thatcher became a member of the backbenches as a

constituency parliamentarian after resigning from the premiership. Her domestic approval rating improved after her resignation; the public opinion was that her leadership had been a plus for the country. At the Age of 66, she retired from the House at the 1992 general election, saying that her departure from the Commons would provide her more freedom to speak her mind.

SHE IS STILL A FORCE TO
RECKON WITH

৩৯৫৩

A t the time of leaving the House of Commons, Thatcher became the premier Prime Minister to set up a foundation, the British wing of the Margaret Thatcher Foundation was later dissolved in 2005 because of financial issues. She authored two volumes of memoirs, The Downing Street Years (1993) and The Path to Power (1995). She and Sir Denis Thatcher her husband relocated to a house in Chester Square in 1991, a residential garden square in Belgravia district in Central London.

৩৯৫৩

THATCHER WAS EMPLOYED by the tobacco company Philip Morris as a "geopolitical consultant" in July 1992, for a fee of $250,000 per year and a yearly contribution of $250,000 to her foundation. Thatcher was paid $50,000 for every speech she delivered.

❧❦❧

In August 1992 she requested for NATO to stop the Serbian attack on Goražde and Sarajevo to end the bloodshed during the Bosnian War. She likened the issue in Bosnia–Herzegovina to "the worst excesses of the Nazis", and hinted that the situation could lead to a "holocaust". She was in total support of Slovenian and Croatian independence. In a 1991 interview for Croatian Radio-television, Thatcher spoke on the Yugoslav Wars; she was against the Western governments for not accepting the breakaway republics of Slovenia and Croatia as independent states and for not providing them with armaments after the invasion of the Serbian-led Yugoslav Army.

❧❦❧

She made various speeches in the Lords challenging the Maastricht Treaty, saying that it was "a treaty too far" and mentioned that "I could never have signed this treaty." She quoted A. V. Dicey when arguing that, as all three main parties were in support of the treaty, the people ought to air their views in a referendum.

❧❦❧

Thatcher was made the honorary chancellor of the College of William & Mary in Virginia from 1993 to 2000, while she also served as chancellor of the private University of Buckingham from 1992 to 1998, a university she had initially opened in 1976 while she was the Education Secretary.

❧❦❧

AFTER TONY BLAIR'S won the election as leader of the
Labour Party in 1994, Thatcher acknowledged Blair as "prob-
ably the most formidable Labour leader since Hugh
Gaitskell", while also commenting that "I see a lot of
socialism behind their front bench, but not in Mr. Blair. I
think he genuinely has moved."Blair responded in like
manner saying that "She was a thoroughly determined person,
and that is an admirable quality".

⚜

IN 1998, Thatcher clamored for the release of ex- Chilean
dictator Augusto Pinochet when Spain arrested him and
prepared to put him on trial for violation of human rights.
She mentioned the help he gave Britain during the Falklands
War. In 1999, she paid him a visit when he was placed under
house arrest close to London. Pinochet was later released in
March 2000 due to his ill health by Jack Straw who was then
Home Secretary.

⚜

AT THE GENERAL election in 2001, Thatcher backed the
Conservative campaign, just like she did in 1992 and 1997, and
in the leadership election of the Conservative party following
its loss, she approved Iain Duncan Smith over Kenneth
Clarke. In 2002 she supported George W. Bush to forcefully
solve the "unfinished business" of Iraq under Saddam Hussein
and hailed Blair for his "strong, bold leadership" in
supporting Bush during the Iraq War.

⚜

SHE RAISED the same issue in her Statecraft: Strategies for a

Changing World, which was published in April 2002 and committed to Ronald Reagan, stating that there would be no peace in the Middle East until Saddam Hussein was removed. Her book also mentioned that Israel must trade land for peace and that the European Union (EU) was a "fundamentally unreformable", "classic utopian project, a monument to the vanity of intellectuals, a programme whose inevitable destiny is failure". She maintained that Britain should revisit its membership terms or else leave the EU and become a member of the North American Free Trade Area.

MARGARET THATCHER EXITS PUBLIC DUTIES DUE TO HEALTH ISSUES

෯෯

A fter suffering several small strokes she was told by her doctors not to involve herself in further public speaking to focus on her health. In March 2002 she made it known publicly that on the advice of her doctors, she would no longer be speaking at public events and cancel all planned speaking engagements that she was scheduled for.

෯෯

ON 26 JUNE 2003, Margaret Thatcher's husband Sir Denis passed away after battling with pancreatic cancer and was cremated on July 3.

෯෯

ON JUNE 11, 2004, Thatcher attended the state funeral service for Ronald Reagan (against the orders of her doctors). She delivered her eulogy through a videotape; due to her health issue, her eulogy message had been pre-recorded several months before. Thatcher traveled to California in the company of the Reagan entourage and attended the memorial service and interment ceremony for Ronald Reagan which took place at the Ronald Reagan Presidential Library.

***

IN 2005, Thatcher condemned the manner in which the decision to attack Iraq had been taken two years before. Although she was still in support of the decision to oust Saddam Hussein from power, she said that (as a scientist by training) she would always be on the lookout for "facts, evidence, and proof", before ordering the armed forces. She celebrated her 80th birthday on October 13 at the Mandarin Oriental Hotel situated in Hyde Park, London; dignitaries in attendance included the Queen, the Duke of Edinburgh, Princess Alexandra, and Tony Blair. Lord Geoffrey Howe of Aberavon was also in attendance and spoke softly of Thatcher saying that

---

"Her real triumph was to have transformed not just one party but two so that when Labour did eventually return, the great bulk of Thatcherism was accepted as irreversible."

***

THATCHER'S DAUGHTER Carol first mentioned that her mother had suffered dementia in 2005, saying "Mum doesn't read much anymore because of her memory loss". In her memoir in 2008, Carol wrote that her mother "could hardly remember the beginning of a sentence by the time she got to the end". She later recounted how she first noticed her mother's dementia when, in conversation, Thatcher couldn't recall the Falklands and Yugoslav conflicts; she mentioned the pain of having to constantly remind her mother on countless occasion that husband Sir Denis Thatcher was dead.

ॐ

IN 2006, Thatcher was in attendance in the US to commemorate the official Washington, D.C. memorial service to mark the fifth anniversary of the September 11 attacks on the US. She was invited as a guest of Vice President Dick Cheney and met with US Secretary of State Condoleezza Rice during her visit. In February 2007 Margaret Thatcher became the first ever British prime minister who was still alive to be honored with a statue in the Houses of Parliament. The bronze statue stands opposite that of her political hero, Sir Winston Churchill, and was presented on February 21, 2007, with Margaret Thatcher in attendance; she mentioned in the Members' Lobby of the Commons that

> "I might have preferred iron – but bronze will do ... It won't rust."

ॐ

THATCHER WAS a public supporter of the Prague Declaration on European Conscience and Communism and the Prague Process that followed and sent a public letter of support to its earlier conference.

THATCHER'S HEALTH
DETERIORATES

❧

A fter Thatcher collapsed at a dinner at the House of
Lords, she suffered low blood pressure and was
admitted to St Thomas' Hospital in central London
on March 7, 2008, for a checkup. In 2009 she was admitted
to the hospital again when she fell down and broke her arm.
In November 2009 Thatcher came back to 10 Downing
street for the presentation of an official portrait by artist
Richard Stone, a remarkable acknowledgment for a living
former Prime Minister. Richard Stone was earlier contracted
to paint portraits of the Queen and Queen Mother.

❧

ON JULY 4, 2011, Thatcher was scheduled to be at a ceremony for the inauguration of a 10 ft (3.0 m) statue of Ronald
Reagan, outside the US Embassy in London, but couldn't
attend due to her ill health. Her last attendance of a sitting of
the House of Lords was on July 19, 2010. The closure of her

office in the House of Lords was announced on July 2011. Prior to the closure of her office in July, Thatcher was acclaimed the most competent Prime Minister of the past 30 years in an Ipsos MORI poll.

BARONESS MARGARET THATCHER passed away on April 8, 2013, aged 87, after battling with a case of stroke. She had been living in a suite at the Ritz Hotel located in London from December 2012 after finding it difficult to deal with the stairs at her Chester Square home in Belgravia. The primary causes of death listed in her death certificate were listed as a "repeated transient ischaemic attack" and a "cerebrovascular accident" while the secondary causes were listed as dementia and a "carcinoma of the bladder".

THE NEWS of her death was met with mixed reactions across the UK; tributes were made in her honor remembering her as Britain's best peaceful and notable Prime Minister. Public celebrations were made to honor her in death to remember her for all the good she did for Britain during her Premiership.

THATCHER HAD MADE KNOWN to her family the Details of her funeral prior to her death. Margaret Thatcher received a ceremonial funeral, which included full military honors, and a church service at St Paul's Cathedral on April 17.

QUEEN ELIZABETH II and the Duke of Edinburgh were in attendance at her funeral, making it the second time the Queen was attending the funeral of any of her former prime ministers; the first being Sir Winston Churchill, who received a state funeral in 1965 with Thatcher in attendance.

❧

AFTER THE MEMORIAL service at St Paul's Cathedral, Margaret Thatcher's body was later cremated at The Mortlake Crematorium, where her husband had earlier been cremated. On September 28, at the All Saints Chapel of the Royal Hospital Chelsea's Margaret Thatcher Infirmary a service for Thatcher was held. In a ceremony with mostly family members in attendance, Thatcher's ashes were interred in the hospital grounds, close to those of her husband Sir Denis Thatcher.

❧ VII ❧

THE THEORY OF
THATCHERISM AND
EFFECTS OF THATCHER'S
POLICIES

֍

Plan your work for today and every day, then work
your plan.
    Margaret Thatcher

֍

Thatcherism was used to describe a systematic and important
change of the post-war consensus, in which the major political parties collectively accepted the central themes of Keyne-
sianism, the welfare state, nationalized industry, and close
running of the economy. The National Health Service was,
however, an exception; with Thatcher promising in 1982 that
it was "safe in our hands". Influenced at the outset by Keith
Joseph, the term Thatcherism was later used to refer to her
policies as well as aspects of her ethical belief and personal

style, including moral tyranny, patriotism, interest in the individual, and a rigid approach to realizing political goals.

❦

Thatcher explained her own political belief in a key and divisive break with the one-nation conservatism of Edward Heath and her Conservative forerunners in an interview which was published in Woman's Own magazine, three months after winning the 1987 general election.

❦

"I think we have gone through a period when too many children and people have been given to understand "I have a problem, it is the Government's job to cope with it!" or "I have a problem, I will go and get a grant to cope with it!" "I am homeless, the Government must house me!" and so they are casting their problems on society and who is society? There is no such thing! There are individual men and women and there are families and no government can do anything except through people and people look to themselves first. It is our duty to look after ourselves and then also to help look after our neighbor and life is a reciprocal business and people have got the entitlements too much in mind without the obligations".

❦

The number of adults who owned shares increased from 7 percent to 25 percent during her tenure as Prime Minister, and more than a million families were able to buy their council houses, giving a rise from 55 percent to 67 percent in owner-occupiers from 1979 to 1990. The houses were given away at a discount of 33–55 per cent, which gave rise to large profits for some of the new home owners. Personal wealth increased by 80 percent in real terms during the 1980s, mainly as a result of an increase in house prices and earnings. Shares in the privatized utilities were given away below their market value to guarantee quick and wide sales, rather than capitalize on national income.

ॐ

Thatcher's reign as Prime Minister also recorded periods of high unemployment and social unrest, and many critics on the opposition of the political spectrum blamed it on her economic procedure for the unemployment rate; many of the areas affected by mass unemployment and her monetarist economic policies remained the same for decades, which resulted in social problems such as drug abuse and family disputes, although this was no fault of Thatcher. Unemployment did not reduce more than the 1979 level during her premiership, although in June 1990 the recorded rate (5.4%) was lower than the rate in April 1979 (5.5%). The long-term effects of her policies on manufacturing remain contentious.

ॐ

Speaking in Scotland in April 2009, Thatcher maintained that she had no regrets and did the right thing by introducing poll tax, and to remove subsidies from "outdated industries, whose markets were in terminal decline", subsidies that created "the culture of dependency, which had done such damage to Britain". Political economist Susan Strange noted the new financial growth model as "casino capitalism", maintaining her stance that speculation and financial trading were becoming more important to the economy than industry.

Critics in the opposition describe her as troublesome and claim she tolerated greed and selfishness. Welsh politician Rhodri Morgan and others have characterized Thatcher as an "overwhelming" figure. Michael White, writing in the New Statesman, questioned the view that her policies had yielded a net profit. Others depict her methods as having been "a mixed bag" or "Curate's egg".

Thatcher did "little to advance the political cause of women" either within her party or the government. Burns stated that some British feminists saw her as "an enemy". June Purvis noted that although Thatcher had fought painstakingly against the sexist injustice of her day prior to her rise to the top, she made no effort to make it easy for other women to get to the top. Thatcher did not see women's rights as needing any particular attention as she did not, particularly during her premiership, believe that women were being dispossessed of their rights. She opted that women should be allowed by default to be allowed to partake in all public appointments but had once proposed that those with young children are supposed to leave the workforce to provide them enough time to take care of their kids without the hassles of working.

Thatcher's notion of immigration in the late 1970s was seen as part of an increasing racist public discussion, which film critic Martin Barker called "new racism". As Leader of the Opposition, Thatcher assumed that the National Front was winning over the large support of Conservative voters with warnings against floods of immigrants. Her plan was to destabilize the Front narrative by asserting that many of their voters had serious challenges which needed to be addressed. In January 1978, Thatcher faulted Labour immigration policy with the aim of swaying voters away from the Front and to the Conservatives. Her expression was followed by a rise in Conservative support to the detriment of the Front. Critics in the opposition reacted in accusing her of being in support of racism. Sociologists Mark Mitchell and Dave Russell in response said that Thatcher had been wrongly misinterpreted, arguing that race was never a major focus of Thatcherism. Throughout her reign as Prime Minister of Britain, both major parties had the same stand on immigration policy, having passed the British Nationality Act in 1981 with bipartisan support. There were no laws passed or proposed by her government focused on limiting immigration, and the talk of race was never mentioned by Thatcher in any of her major speeches during her premiership.

⚜

Many of Thatcher's policies influenced the Labour Party, which came back to power in 1997 under the premiership of Tony Blair. Tony Blair changed the party to "New Labour" in 1994 with the aim of increasing its outlook beyond its usual supporters, and to attract those who had backed Thatcher, such as the "Essex man". Thatcher had made it known that she saw the New Labour Party as her greatest achievement.

⚜

After the death of Thatcher, Scottish First Minister Alex Salmond argued that her agendas had the "unintended consequence" of supporting Scottish devolution. On Scotland Tonight, Lord Foulkes of Cumnock agreed that Thatcher had provided the momentum for devolution. Writing for The Scotsman, Thatcher was strongly against devolution on the grounds that it would ultimately lead to Scottish independence

☙❧

Thatcher's was British Prime Minister for a period of 11 years and 209 days this made her the longest Prime Minister since Lord Salisbury whose Premiership span a period of 13 years and 252 days, and the longest continuous reign in office since Lord Liverpool who spent 14 years and 305 days. She was the longest-serving Prime Minister and was officially referred to as such, as the position was only officially given acknowledgment in the order of superiority in 1905.

❧ VIII ☙
MARGARET THATCHER'S RECOGNITIONS

❦

I always cheer up immensely if an attack is particularly wounding because I think, well, if they attack one personally, it means they have not a single political argument left.

Margaret Thatcher

❦

Having led her party to victory three times at the general election (three times in a row and twice in a landslide victory), she is ranked as the most popular party leader in history of Britain in regards to the number of votes cast for the winning party, with more than 40 million ballots cast for the Conservative Party in total between the period of 1979 and 1987. Her final election win was welcomed as a "historic hat trick" by The Independent and other major newspaper publications.

❧

Thatcher was voted as the fourth-greatest Prime Minister of the 20th century in a poll conducted by 139 academics which was organized by MORI, and in 2002 she was ranked highest among living persons in the BBC poll 100 Greatest Britons. Time magazine in 1999 hailed Thatcher as one of the 100 most important people of the 20th century. In 2015 she led a poll organized by Scottish Widows, a chief financial services company, as the most influential woman of the last two centuries; and in 2016 she topped BBC Radio 4's Woman's Hour Power List of women believed to have had the most impact on female lives during the past 70 years.

❧

Margaret Thatcher became a Privy Councillor (PC) on emerging as the Secretary of State for Education and Science in 1970. She was the first woman permitted to full membership rights as an honorary member of the Carlton Club on emerging as Leader of the Conservative Party in 1975.

❧

During her premiership, Thatcher was acknowledged with two honorary distinctions:

- Invited to become an Honorary Fellow of the Royal Institute of Chemistry (FRIC) on October 24, 1979

- Elected a Fellow of the Royal Society (FRS), a point of controversy among some of the then-existing Fellows on July 1, 1983
- Ribbon bars
- Ribbon of the Order of Merit
- United Kingdom Order of Merit (1990)
- Ribbon of the Order of Good Hope
- South Africa Order of Good Hope (1991)
- Ribbon of the Presidential Medal of Freedom
- United States Presidential Medal of Freedom (1993)
- Ribbon of the Order of the Garter
- United Kingdom Order of the Garter (1995)

At about two weeks after her resignation, Thatcher was appointed as a Member of the Order of Merit (OM) by Queen Elizabeth II in December 1990. Her husband Denis was honored with a hereditary baronetcy during the ceremony. As the wife of a knight, Thatcher was permitted to use the honorific title "Lady", a title she was allowed to use but refused to use. She accepted to be accorded as Lady Thatcher in her own right in 1992 when she was admitted into the order of nobility in the House of Lords.

❦

Thatcher was presented with the highest civilian awards of the United States and South Africa in 1999:

- The Presidential Medal of Freedom on behalf of President George H. W. Bush on March 7, 1991
- The Grand Cross of the Order of Good Hope on behalf of President F. W. de Klerk on May 15, 1991

- Margaret Thatcher Day was marked in the Falklands every January 10 since 1992. In celebration of her first visit to the Islands in January 1983, 6 months after the end of the Falklands War in June 1982.

❧❧

In 1992, Thatcher was made a member of the House of Lords which earned her the title of Baroness Thatcher, of Kesteven in the County of Lincolnshire. As a Baroness, Thatcher was permitted to use a personal coat of arms. Another coat of arms was made for Thatcher after she was appointed as a Lady Companion of the Order of the Garter (LG) in 1995, the highest order of chivalry for women. Despite having been permitted to use her own arms, Thatcher occasionally made use of the Royal Arms in place of her own against protocol.

AFTERWORD

༺✿༻

What is success? I think it is a mixture of having a flair for the thing that you are doing; knowing that it is not enough, that you have got to have hard work and a certain sense of purpose.

Margaret Thatcher

༺✿༻

The life of Margaret Thatcher was one devoted to selfless service, she was more concerned with being the voice of the people, which was evident in her many exploits in Britain and outside Britain. Her disdain for apartheid in the 80s and 90s earned her international recognition during her premiership. Thatcher stood for the truth and just like every great leader most of her policies wasn't welcomed by everyone especially the opposition. As leader of the opposition she stood firm even when it seemed like the political scene which was dominated by the male folks wasn't ready to welcome a female into the top positions of leadership. But Thatcher warmed her way into the hearts of everyone who believed in the conservative ideas she strongly supported. As a leader she was feared and respected and didn't allow herself to be intimidated by distractions from the opposition. Thatcher was equally brave, this was evident when an assassination attempt was made on her life, but not only did she survive the attempt she went ahead to continue with the planned event in the same place where the plot to assassinate her was carried out. This goes to show that she was a leader who wasn't going to be distracted from her work.

⚜

Margaret Thatcher lived an exemplary life that is worthy of emulation especially in respect to her regard for the liberation of the common man, and the implementation of policies that will lead to economic development.

Margaret Thatcher's Strengths

One of Thatcher's greatest strength was her leadership style; the ability for her to be committed to service even in the midst of distractions is an attribute that is highly laudable. An important aspect of her leadership style was her determined, tenacious and steadfast which is common mostly among revolutionary leaders.

Margaret Thatchers Weaknesses

It is often said that Thatcher's strengths was also her weaknesses in the sense that she could occasionally be stubborn, obstinate and uncompromising, with many economist calling her as a control freak. He refusal to yield to pressure was often conceived as her been always in the need to be in control.

❁

Her unwillingness to consider the opinions of others was partly what led to the end of her premiership. Her handling of the new local taxation system which was called the Poll Tax didn't really go down well with key cabinet members and majority of the public. Even when Ministers in her cabinet advised and warned her that the policy would backfire, she pushed forward and remained committed to implementing the policy. Unfortunately, the policy sparked violent public protests which affected her approval ratings negatively which led to her exit from the premiership.

❁

Qualities we can imbibe from Margaret Thatcher's Strength in our Daily lives.

❁

Passion

Margaret Thatcher had a great passion for her country and the people she was leading. She believed strongly in the privatisation and freedom. This passion made her to push forward to enact key policies even in the midst of distractions. Her passion for the emancipation of the people made her to fight to achieve many of her key policies which she always won.

We can learn from Margaret Thatcher's passion for service by loving what we do and be committed to achieving our goals. When we are passionate about our endeavours it goes a great deal in helping to realise our goals even in the midst of distractions and setbacks.

Determination

Thatcher's determination to realise her goals played a major role in her leadership. She was happy and willing to fight for what she believed was right for the growth of the country. Her determination to fight the tyranny of the USSR played a major role in ending the Soviet Union.

With determination to succeed half of the job is done already, because you have told yourself that irrespective of what comes your way you are happy and willing to confront it. It doesn't matter if your goal is to succeed in business or politics or even in your personal endeavors with a strong determination, you can be certain of achieving your goals.

Confidence

Margaret Thatcher showed strong confidence in herself and her beliefs, she wasn't going to be swayed easily by the opposition. She commanded respect all throughout the period she represented her country at different stages. This made her a voice people were willing to listen to all over Britain and outside Britain. She believed in her ability to see things through even when others didn't.

Self confidence is an important attribute if you want to succeed in whatever you aim to achieve. When you believe in yourself, you don't care what the circumstances or challenges are, you trust that you will always emerge victorious.

Brave

Margaret Thatcher showed bravery all through her leadership of Britain. She was outspoken and wasn't intimidated. She wasn't scared of challenging tyranny especially of the Soviet Union. Another time Margaret Thatcher showed bravery was when an assassination attempt was made on her life at a planned Conservative Conference at a hotel. She was brave enough to escape without injuries and returned the next day to attend the conference at the same hotel.

Been able to be brave even in the midst of fear and tension is important to moving ahead in life. There are a lot of instances where we have to be brave in order to move forward. Face your fears and conquer them if you want to succeed in life.

Selfless Service

Throughout the period of Margaret Thatcher reign, she wasn't bothered with enriching herself and was concerned with liberating the people. She wasn't interested in personal gains and her integrity was never questioned. This fact alone cannot be said of many world leaders.

We should focus more on rendering services that will be beneficial to others than ourselves. We should not bother ourselves with how much we stand to make, but how much we stand to change.

OTHER BOOKS ON MARGARET THATCHER

❧

O ther Books on Margaret Thatcher for
further reading.

❧

Not for Turning by Robin Harris

❧

Margaret Thatcher, Volume one: The Grocer's
Daughter by John Campbell

❧

Power and Personality by Jonathan Aitken's

YOUR FREE EBOOK!

As a way of saying thank you for reading our book, we're offering you a free copy of the below eBook.

Happy Reading!

GO WWW.THEHISTORYHOUR.COM/CLEO/

Manufactured by Amazon.ca
Bolton, ON

16650671R00053